Tajweed Untangled

The clear-cut guide to learning the art of Quran recitation.

First published in the United Kingdom in 1431 AH (2010 CE) by
Learning Roots Ltd.
Unit 6, TGEC, Town Hall Approach Road, London , N15 4RX.
www.learningroots.com

Reprinted in 1432 AH (2011 CE) and twice in 1433 AH (2012 CE).

Copyright © Learning Roots 2010
Authored by Yasmin Mussa and Zaheer Khatri.
Cover design, layout & illustrations by the Learning Roots Education
Design Service.

Acknowledgements
The publisher thanks Allah ﷻ, Lord of the Worlds, for making this
publication possible.

British Library Cataloguing in Publication Data
A CIP catalogue record for this book is available from the British Library.
Printed and bound in Turkey.
ISBN: 978-1-905516-31-5

Contents

Introduction

All praise is due to Allah ﷻ, the One who revealed His book and praised the ones who recite it and act upon it:

Surah Fātir: 29

Verily, those who recite the Book of Allah and establish the prayer and spend (in charity) out of what We have provided for them, secretly and openly, hope for a (sure) trade gain that will never perish.

﴿ إِنَّ ٱلَّذِينَ يَتْلُونَ كِتَٰبَ ٱللَّهِ وَأَقَامُواْ ٱلصَّلَوٰةَ وَأَنفَقُواْ مِمَّا رَزَقْنَٰهُمْ سِرًّا وَعَلَانِيَةً يَرْجُونَ تِجَٰرَةً لَّن تَبُورَ ۝ ﴾

And may the peace and blessings of Allah ﷻ be upon the final Prophet, Muhammad ﷺ, the best of creation, the one to whom was revealed the Book of Allah ﷻ and from it the verse:

Surah Al-Muzzammil: 4

Or a little more; and recite the Quran in slow, measured, rhythmic tones.

﴿ أَوْ زِدْ عَلَيْهِ وَرَتِّلِ ٱلْقُرْءَانَ تَرْتِيلًا ۝ ﴾

And from the Prophet's ﷺ beautiful traditions, we find the words:

Abu Dawud

Narrated on the authority of Al-Bara' Ibn Azib ﷺ.

> *"Beautify the Quran with your voices."*

He ﷺ also explained the immense rewards prepared for those who recite the Quran with sincerity:

At-Tirmidhi

Narrated on the authority of Abdullah Ibn Mas'oud ﷺ.

> *"Whoever recites one letter of the Book of Allah, for him will be one hasanah (blessing); and one hasanah is worth ten others. I do not say that Alif-Lām-Meem is one letter, but alif is one letter, lām is one letter and meem is one letter."*

Muslim

Narrated on the authority of Aa'isha ﷺ.

> *"One who recites the Quran and is well versed in it (i.e. its recitation), will be in the company of Angels who are scribes, noble and righteous; and one who falters in its recitation and has to exert himself, will get double the reward."*

Learning the art of its recital is from the most honoured studies due to its relation to the Book of Allah ﷻ:

Bukhari

Narrated on the authority of 'Uthman ﷺ.

> *"The best of you is the one who learns the Quran and teaches it."*

Hence we arrive at the study of *tajweed* which linguistically means 'to do something well'. The word *tajweed* however, carries a more specific meaning when used in relation to the Quran. To recite the Book of Allah ﷻ with *tajweed* means to give every letter its right by making sure they are pronounced properly with their specific characteristics. In other words, *tajweed* of the Quran means to recite every letter in the exact way it was revealed to the Prophet Muhammed ﷺ:

Muslim

Aa'isha ﷺ said, "The Prophet ﷺ used to recite the chapter slowly, so much so that it would be longer than (other) chapters that were actually longer than it."

Bukhari

Anas ﷺ was asked about the recitation of the Messenger of Allah ﷺ, so he replied, "He used to elongate the letters."

Ahmad, Abu Dawud and At-Tirmidhi

Umm Salamah ﷺ, the wife of the Prophet ﷺ was asked about the recitation of the Messenger of Allah ﷺ, so she said, "He used to pause in his recitation, verse by verse."

Learning to recite the Quran with *tajweed* includes the study of where the sound of each letter originates, the characteristics and the rules of how these sounds change according to the order in which the letters occur. However, *tajweed* is not just an academic study and so knowledge of the rules is not enough to gain mastery of the subject. As the following chapter explains, there are a number of requirements that must be met in order for *tajweed* to be learned effectively.

Prerequisites

Learning to recite the Quran is a noble act of worship for which the intention should only be for Allah ﷻ. After this crucial prerequisite, you will also need to address the following matters before you begin:

- **A Proficient Teacher:** *Tajweed* can only be effectively learned under the guidance of a proficient teacher whose correct pronounciation is emulated and feedback is offered, thus coaching the student to mastery of the sounds. This book assumes the presence of a well versed teacher who shall recite the examples in the 'Study' section at the beginning of most chapters, and listen to students recite the practice lines after the rules have been explained.

- **Arabic Alphabet:** You should be able to identify each letter of the Arabic alphabet and pronounce it. Your pronounciation need not be accurate or perfect to begin with, but a general awareness and ability to read letters is essential.

- **Read Harakāt:** You should be able to identify the various markings on the letters such as the short vowels, *tanween*, *sukoon* and *shaddah* to understand the effect each of these have when applied to a letter.

- **Read Arabic:** If you are able to read the Arabic alphabet and understand the functions of the *harakāt*, you should have the ability to read Arabic text. Your reading does not need to be proficient to begin with, but you should have some ability to accurately read words and sentences.

◌َ	◌ُ	◌ْ
....	....	....	....
	◌َ		
◌ً		◌ٌ	◌ٍ
....	....	....	....
	◌ً		

ث	ت	ب	أ
د	خ	ح	ج
س	ز	ر	ذ
ط	ض	ص	ش
ف	غ	ع	ظ
م	ل	ك	ق
ى	و	ه	ن

Sound Origins

The study of *tajweed* typically begins with the origins of the letter sounds. This is known as *makhārij-ul huroof* (مخارج الحروف) and forms the foundation of your *tajweed* skills.

Study

Listen and repeat each of the following words and try to locate which area of your voice passage each sound is coming from.

Group 1

إِخْ إِغْ إِحْ إِعْ إِهْ إِءْ

Group 2

إِنْ إِطْ إِسْ إِجْ إِكْ إِقْ

إِضْ إِيْ إِذْ إِتْ إِلْ إِرْ

إِثْ إِذْ إِشْ إِزْ إِصْ إِظْ

Group 3

إِفْ إِبْ إِمْ إِوْ

You may have noticed that the sounds from each group originate from different places along your voice passage. In particular, you may have noted that:

- Sounds from Group 1 all originate from the **throat**.
- Sounds from Group 2 all originate from the **tongue**.
- Sounds from Group 3 all originate from the **lips**.

The part of the voice passage from which a sound originates is called *makhraj* (مخرج), the plural of which is *makhārij* (مخارج). In addition to the three *makhārij* mentioned above, there are two other areas from which sounds originate. They are:

- **Nasal Passage;** from which the *ghunnah* (غنّة) sound originates.
- **Chest;** from which the long vowel sounds of (ا), (و) and (ی) originate.

Reference

Nasal sounds are discussed in the chapter entitled 'Ghunnah' on page 50 and the chest sounds are discussed in the chapters on madd sounds which begin from page 66.

Although these two areas do not relate to specific letters, they are related to other important sounds. We shall revisit these areas in more detail later, but for now it is enough for you to understand the rule below.

Rule

When reciting the Noble Quran, all sounds originate from one of the following five general areas:

1. Throat
2. Chest
3. Tongue
4. Nasal Passage
5. Lips

Label the diagram below showing the five general *makhārij* and the letters that originate from them. Some boxes have been filled in for you.

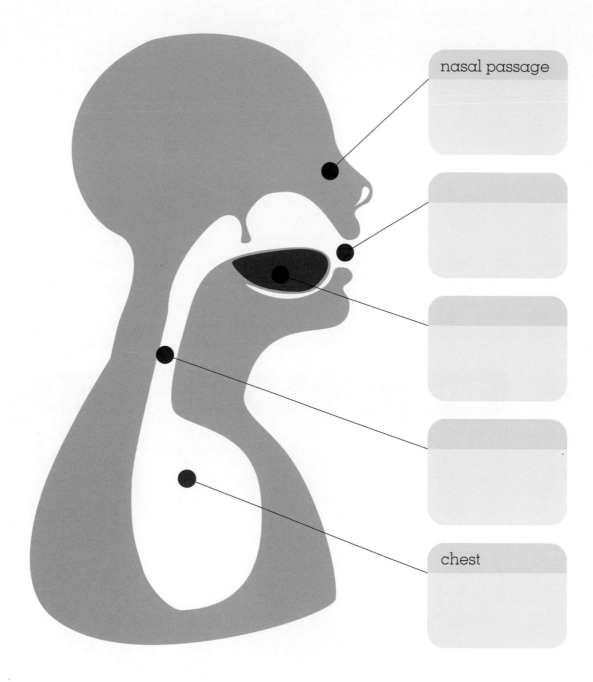

nasal passage

chest

Study

Listen and repeat each of the following sounds again. Within each group of letters, do the sounds originate from exactly the same place in the *makhraj*?

Throat

إِخْ	إِغْ	إِحْ	إِعْ	إِهْ	إِءْ

Tongue

إِنْ	إِطْ	إِسْ	إِجْ	إِكْ	إِقْ
إِضْ	إِيْ	إِدْ	إِثْ	إِلْ	إِرْ
إِثْ	إِذْ	إِشْ	إِزْ	إِصْ	إِظْ

Lips

إِوْ	إِمْ	إِبْ	إِفْ

Reflect

You may have noticed that even within each of the groups above, sounds do not all originate from exactly the same place. For example, in the tongue group, there are some sounds that originate from the tip, some from the middle and some from the back of the tongue. In the chapters that follow, we shall study the general *makhārij* more closely to locate the point of origin of each letter precisely.

Throat

Study

Listen and repeat each of the letters of the throat below. Try to locate which area of the throat each sound is coming from.

Group 1

إِءْ   إِءْ

Group 2

إِغْ   إِحْ

Group 3

إِغْ   إِخْ

Reflect

You may have noticed that the sounds from each group of letters originate from different places along your throat. In particular, you may have noted that:

- Sounds from Group 1 all originate from the **lower area** of the throat.
- Sounds from Group 2 all originate from the **mid-area** of the throat.
- Sounds from Group 3 all originate from the **upper area** of the throat.

Task

Label the diagram below showing the three specific *makhārij* of the throat and the letters that originate from them.

Rule

The throat has three specific *makhārij*. Each one of these *makhārij* relate to two specific letters, summarised by the table below.

Makhraj	Related Letters	
Lower Throat	ء	ه
Mid-Throat	ع	ح
Upper Throat	غ	خ

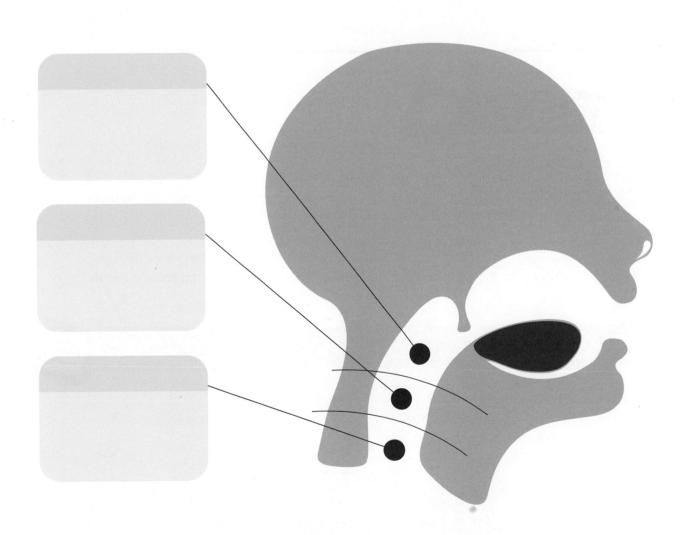

Lips

Study

Listen and repeat each of the letters of the lips below. Try to locate which area of the lips each sound is coming from.

Group 1

إِبْ   إِمْ   إِوْ

Group 2

إِفْ

Reflect

You may have noticed that the sounds from each group of letters originate from different places on your lips. In particular, you may have noted that:

- Sounds from Group 1 all originate from **between the lips**.
- The sound from Group 2 originates from the **inside-lower lip**.

Rule

The lips have two specific *makhārij*. One *makhraj* relates to three letters while the other relates to just one letter.

Makhraj	Related Letters		
Between the Lips	ب	م	و
Inside-Lower Lip	ف		

Label the diagram below showing the two specific *makhārij* of the lips and the letters that originate from them.

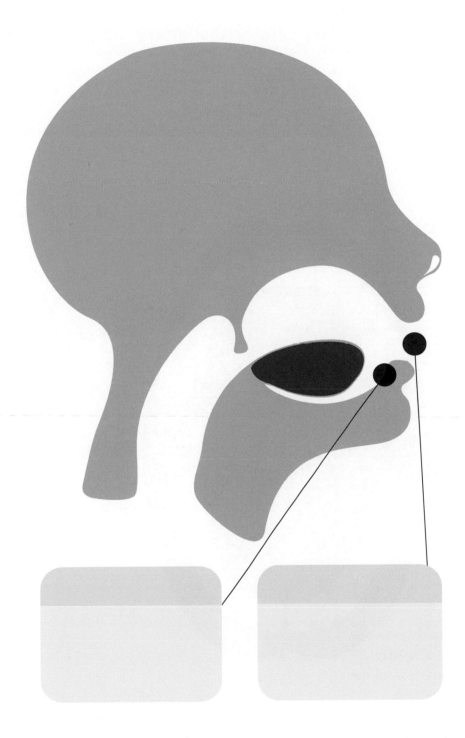

Tongue

The tongue is the main organ of speech, and so it is no surprise that the majority of sounds originate from it. Unlike the throat and lips, the specific *makhārij* of the tongue are very intricate and are more difficult to locate precisely. In order to describe these *makhārij* clearly, it is necessary to know the names of the different parts of the tongue and the teeth that it touches when producing sound. The diagram below will help you describe the *makhārij* more accurately.

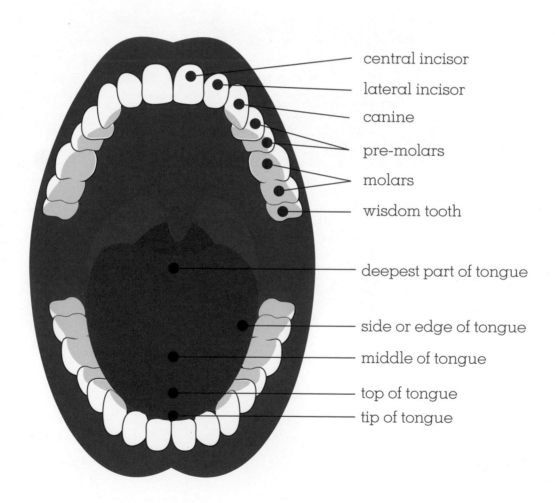

central incisor

lateral incisor

canine

pre-molars

molars

wisdom tooth

deepest part of tongue

side or edge of tongue

middle of tongue

top of tongue

tip of tongue

Study

Listen and repeat the letters of the tongue below. Try to locate which area of the tongue each sound is coming from as it interacts with the mouth and teeth.

Group 1

إِقْ

Group 2

إِكْ

Group 3

إِجْ   إِشْ   إِيْ

Group 4

إِضْ

Group 5

إِلْ

Group 6

إِنْ

Group 7

إِرْ

Group 8

إِثْ   إِدْ   إِطْ

Group 9

إِزْ   إِسْ   إِضْ

Group 10

إِثْ   إِذْ   إِظْ

You may have noticed that the sounds from each group of letters originate from different places on your tongue. In particular, you may have noticed:

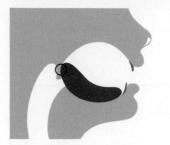

The sound from Group 1 originates from the **extreme back of the tongue when touching the palate.**

The sound from Group 2 originates from the **back of the tongue when touching the palate.**

The sounds from Group 3 originate from the **middle of the tongue when touching palate.**

The sound from Group 4 originates from the **back edge of the tongue, upturned as it touches the molar teeth.**

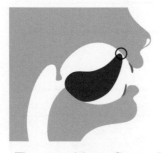

The sound from Group 5 originates from **between the edge of the tongue when it touches the gums behind the incisors, canines and pre-molar teeth.**

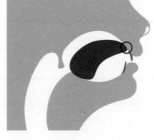

The sound from Group 6 originates from **between the tip of the tongue when it touches the gums behind the central incisors.**

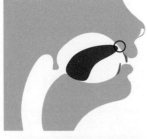

The sound from Group 7 originates from **the tip of the tongue, with the top of the tip close to the gums behind the central incisors.**

 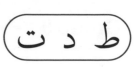

The sounds from Group 8 originate from the **tip of the tongue along with its upper surface touching the roots of the central incisors.**

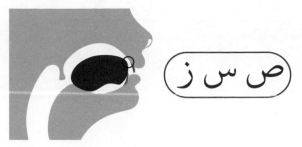

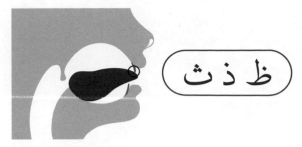

The sounds from Group 9 originate from **between the tip of the tongue and the plates near the central incisors.**

The sounds from Group 10 originate from **the tip of the tongue when touching the bottom edge of the central incisors.**

Rule

The tongue has ten specific *makhārij*. Four of these *makhārij* relate to three letters each, while the other six relate to just one letter each.

Makhraj	Related Letters
Extreme back of the tongue when touching the palate.	ق
Back of the tongue when touching the palate.	ك
Middle of the tongue when touching the palate.	ي ش ج
Back edge of the tongue, upturned as it touches the molar teeth.	ض
Between the edge of the tongue when it touches the gums behind the incisors, canines and pre-molar teeth.	ل
Between the tip of the tongue when it touches the gums behind the central incisors.	ن
The tip of the tongue, with the top of the tip close to the gums behind the central incisors.	ر
The tip of the tongue along with its upper surface touching the roots of the central incisors.	ط د ت
Between the tip of the tongue and the plates near the central incisors.	ص س ز
The tip of the tongue when touching the bottom edge of the central incisors.	ظ ذ ث

Origins Summary

Remember that we first identified five general areas from which sounds originate. They were:

1. Throat
2. Lips
3. Tongue

_____

4. Nasal Passage
5. Chest

Out of these five *makhārij*, we now know that the first three (throat, lips and tongue) can be further divided into specific areas from which sounds of letters originate. The remaining two (chest and nasal passage) do not relate to letters and are not divided into specific areas, as summarised by the following two rules:

Rule

The nasal passage is one *makhraj*, containing the sound of *ghunnah* (غَنَّة) which is not a letter, but a nasal sound.

Rule

The chest is one *makhraj*, containing the sound of the long vowel sounds (ا), (و) and (ى).

With the *makhārij* of the nasal passage and chest explained, we can now summarise all of the *makhārij*.

Complete the table below, summarising the *makhārij* of all the letters and sounds used during Quran recitation.

Region	Specific Makhraj	Related Letters		
	Chest			
	Lower throat			
	Upper throat			
	Extreme back of the tongue when touching the palate.			
	Back of the tongue when touching the palate.			
	Middle of the tongue when touching the palate.			
	Back edge of the tongue, upturned as it touches the molar teeth.			
	Between the edge of the tongue when it touches the gums behind the incisors, canines and pre-molar teeth.			
	Between the tip of the tongue when it touches the gums behind the central incisors.			
	The tip of the tongue, with the top of the tip close to the gums behind the central incisors.			
	The tip of the tongue along with its upper surface touching the roots of the central incisors.			
	Between the tip of the tongue and the plates near the central incisors.			
	The tip of the tongue when touching the bottom edge of the central incisors.			
	Between the Lips			
Nasal Passage				
Total	17			

Characteristics

Study

Listen and repeat each of the following letters. What do you notice about the *makhraj* and sound of the letters in each group?

Group 1

ت ط

Group 2

ذ ظ

Reflect

You may have noticed that the *makhraj* of the letters in Group 1 was the same, yet they both sound different. For example the letter (ط) has a heavy sound compared to the softer sounding (ت). The same could be said for the letters in Group 2 where the letter (ظ) sounds distinctly heavier than (ذ). This tells us that while studying the *makhārij* of letters is very helpful, we still need to understand more about the letters in order to pronounce them correctly.

Reference
The chapter entitled 'Tafkheem & Tarqeeq' begins on page 36 and 'Qalqalah' begins on page 46.

The way in which we can tell the difference between these letters is through a study of their characteristics or *sifāt* (صفات). *Sifāt* is one of the most advanced topics in the science of *tajweed*. There are over twenty different characteristics and each letter has at least four of them. We will not cover all the *sifāt* in detail, but we will mention some of them in the forthcoming chapters entitled *Tafkheem & Tarqeeq* and *Qalqalah*.

Seeking Refuge

Allah ﷺ says in His Noble Book:

﴾ فَإِذَا قَرَأْتَ ٱلْقُرْءَانَ فَٱسْتَعِذْ بِٱللَّهِ مِنَ ٱلشَّيْطَٰنِ ٱلرَّجِيمِ ﴿٩٨﴾ ﴾

Surah Nahl: 98

And when you recite the Quran, seek refuge in Allah from satan the outcast.

In following this command from our Creator, we must ask Allah ﷺ to protect us from *shaytān* the outcast. This seeking of protection is known as *al-isti'ātha* (الاستعاذة) and is performed by saying the following words:

أَعُوذُ بِاللهِ مِنَ الشَّيْطَانِ الرَّجِيمِ

Quick Question

Do you know of another version of the isti'ātha?.

The meaning of which is *'I seek refuge in Allah from shaytān the outcast.'*

Task

What are some of the benefits from seeking refuge in Allah ﷺ before reciting?

....

....

....

....

....

....

Rule

Seeking refuge should be done before beginning any recitation of the Quran and should be repeated if you are interrupted during your recitation by necessary conversation, work or other such incidents.

Basmalah

Rule

After seeking refuge in Allah ﷻ, we recite the *basmalah* (البسملة) by saying:

بِسْمِ ٱللَّهِ ٱلرَّحْمَـٰنِ ٱلرَّحِيمِ

This statement translates as *'I begin in the name of Allah the Merciful, the Bestower of Mercy.'* The *basmalah* must be recited at the beginning of every chapter of the Quran.

Exception to the Rule
The only exception to this rule is the beginning of Sūrah At-Tawbah where you seek refuge in Allah ﷻ, and continue on to recite the first verse without saying the basmalah in between.

Study

Listen and repeat each of the followng verses. Take care to note how the verses are connected during the recitation.

Example 1

﴿ قُلْ هُوَ ٱللَّهُ أَحَدٌ ۝ ﴾ ⬤ ﴿ بِسْمِ ٱللَّهِ ٱلرَّحْمَـٰنِ ٱلرَّحِيمِ ۝ ﴾ ⬤ ﴿ فِى جِيدِهَا حَبْلٌ مِّن مَّسَدٍ ۝ ﴾

Example 2

﴿ قُلْ هُوَ ٱللَّهُ أَحَدٌ ۝ ﴾ ⬅ ﴿ بِسْمِ ٱللَّهِ ٱلرَّحْمَـٰنِ ٱلرَّحِيمِ ۝ ﴾ ⬅ ﴿ فِى جِيدِهَا حَبْلٌ مِّن مَّسَدٍ ۝ ﴾

Example 3

﴿ قُلْ هُوَ ٱللَّهُ أَحَدٌ ۝ ﴾ ⬅ ﴿ بِسْمِ ٱللَّهِ ٱلرَّحْمَـٰنِ ٱلرَّحِيمِ ۝ ﴾ ⬤ ﴿ فِى جِيدِهَا حَبْلٌ مِّن مَّسَدٍ ۝ ﴾

Reflect

You may have noticed that there was a difference in each of the examples in the way in which the verses were connected with the *basmalah*. In particular you may have noticed that:

- In Example 1, each verse was seperated from the *basmalah*.
- In Example 2, there was no break in the recitation, and so the two verses and the *basmalah* were recited in one breath.
- In Example 3, there was a stop between the final verse of the previous *sūrah* and the *basmalah*. Then the *basmalah* was recited with the first verse of the next *sūrah* without a break.

Rule

When reciting the *basmalah* between the last verse of a *sūrah* and the first verse of the next, there are three ways in which the recitation can proceed:

- There is a stop between the last verse, the *basmalah* and the first verse.
- There is no break in the last verse, the *basmalah* and the first verse.
- There is a stop between the last verse, the *basmalah*, but no stop between the *basmalah* and the first verse.

Task

Which of the following combination of stops and connections is not allowed, and why do you think this is so?

....
﴿ فِى جِيدِهَا حَبْلٌ مِّن مَّسَدٍ ۝ ﴾ ⬤ ﴿ بِسْمِ ٱللَّهِ ٱلرَّحْمَٰنِ ٱلرَّحِيمِ ۝ ﴾ ⬤ ﴿ قُلْ هُوَ ٱللَّهُ أَحَدٌ ۝ ﴾

....
﴿ فِى جِيدِهَا حَبْلٌ مِّن مَّسَدٍ ۝ ﴾ ⬤ ﴿ بِسْمِ ٱللَّهِ ٱلرَّحْمَٰنِ ٱلرَّحِيمِ ۝ ﴾ ⬅ ﴿ قُلْ هُوَ ٱللَّهُ أَحَدٌ ۝ ﴾

....
﴿ فِى جِيدِهَا حَبْلٌ مِّن مَّسَدٍ ۝ ﴾ ⬅ ﴿ بِسْمِ ٱللَّهِ ٱلرَّحْمَٰنِ ٱلرَّحِيمِ ۝ ﴾ ⬅ ﴿ قُلْ هُوَ ٱللَّهُ أَحَدٌ ۝ ﴾

....
﴿ فِى جِيدِهَا حَبْلٌ مِّن مَّسَدٍ ۝ ﴾ ⬅ ﴿ بِسْمِ ٱللَّهِ ٱلرَّحْمَٰنِ ٱلرَّحِيمِ ۝ ﴾ ⬤ ﴿ قُلْ هُوَ ٱللَّهُ أَحَدٌ ۝ ﴾

Stop Symbols

Knowing the correct points at which to stop or continue during recitation is important in order not to distort the meaning of the verses. The printed copy of the Quran, known as *mus-haf* (المصحف), carries symbols that help the reciter identify the points at which to stop or continue. We shall look closely at these symbols and their meanings in this chapter.

Study

Listen and repeat each of the following verses. Note the points at which breaks in the recitation occur or do not occur.

Example 1

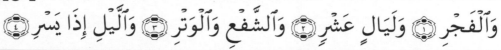

Example 2

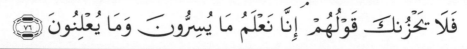

Example 3

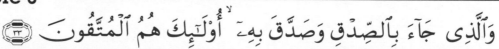

Example 4

Reflect

You may have noticed that in Example 1, the recitation stopped at the end of each verse. The symbol for the end of each verse is (⊙). It is from the Prophetic *Sunnah* to stop at the end of each verse:

*Umm Salamah ⌖, the wife of the Prophet ⌖ was asked about the
recitation of the Messenger of Allah ⌖, so she said, "He used to pause
in his recitation, verse by verse."*

In Example 2 you may have noticed that there is a break in the recitation at
the point where the symbol (⌖) occurred. At this symbol, it is compulsory to
stop in order to avoid altering the meaning.

In Example 3 you may have noticed that the recitation continued at the
point where the symbol (ﻻ) occurred. It is not allowed to stop at this symbol,
and so you must continue reciting past this symbol without a break.

In Example 4, you may have noticed that there were two (⁖) symbols. These
symbols always occur in pairs. You should stop at either one of these
symbols, but not both.

In addition to the symbols mentioned above there are others that are found
in the *mus-haf*. The table contained in the rule below summarises some of
the different kinds of symbols found.

Rule

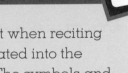

Since knowing where to stop or continue is important when reciting
the Quran, a printed *mus-haf* contains symbols integrated into the
script to help the reciter follow the laws of stopping. The symbols and
their meanings are as follows:

	Meaning
۝	End of ayah; stop recommended.
مـ	Compulsory stop.
ج	Permissible to stop.
صلے	Permissible to stop but preferable to continue.
قلے	Permissible to continue but preferable to stop.
ﻻ	Prohibited to stop.
⁖ ⁖	Stop at either of these two symbols but not both.

Task

Mushaf Scripts

The examples of stop symbols shown in this book are based on the 'Uthmani calligraphic script. One of the other most common scripts is the Majdi script, in which the symbols differ in both form and meaning. Hence it is important to acquaint yourself with the particulars of the script used in your personal mushaf.

The stop symbols and their meanings may differ from one printed *mus-haf* to another. An explanation of the stop symbols used in a *mus-haf* can usually be found in the last few pages. Find this page in your personal *mus-haf* and record the different types of symbols and their meanings in the table below.

Symbol	Meaning

Read the following verses, taking care to stop or continue your recitation at the appropriate symbol.

Line 1

﴿ هَـٰذَا يَوْمُ ٱلْفَصْلِ ۖ جَمَعْنَـٰكُمْ وَٱلْأَوَّلِينَ ﴿٣٨﴾ ﴾

Line 2

﴿ ٱلسَّمَآءُ مُنفَطِرٌ بِهِ ۚ كَانَ وَعْدُهُۥ مَفْعُولًا ﴿١٨﴾ ﴾

Line 3

﴿ وَلَا يَتَمَنَّوْنَهُۥ أَبَدًا بِمَا قَدَّمَتْ أَيْدِيهِمْ ۚ وَٱللَّهُ عَلِيمٌۢ بِٱلظَّـٰلِمِينَ ﴿٧﴾ ﴾

Line 4

﴿ قُلْ إِن كُنتُمْ تُحِبُّونَ ٱللَّهَ فَٱتَّبِعُونِى يُحْبِبْكُمُ ٱللَّهُ وَيَغْفِرْ لَكُمْ ذُنُوبَكُمْ ۗ وَٱللَّهُ غَفُورٌ رَّحِيمٌ ﴿٣١﴾ ﴾

Line 5

﴿ ۞ فَـَٔامَنَ لَهُۥ لُوطٌ ۘ وَقَالَ إِنِّى مُهَاجِرٌ إِلَىٰ رَبِّى ۚ إِنَّهُۥ هُوَ ٱلْعَزِيزُ ٱلْحَكِيمُ ﴿٢٦﴾ ﴾

Line 6

﴿ وَعَدَ ٱللَّهُ ٱلَّذِينَ ءَامَنُوا۟ وَعَمِلُوا۟ ٱلصَّـٰلِحَـٰتِ ۙ لَهُم مَّغْفِرَةٌ وَأَجْرٌ عَظِيمٌ ﴿٩﴾ ﴾

Line 7

﴿ أَلَمْ يَأْتِكُمْ نَبَؤُا۟ ٱلَّذِينَ مِن قَبْلِكُمْ قَوْمِ نُوحٍ وَعَادٍ وَثَمُودَ ۛ وَٱلَّذِينَ مِنۢ بَعْدِهِمْ ۛ لَا يَعْلَمُهُمْ إِلَّا ٱللَّهُ ۚ جَآءَتْهُمْ رُسُلُهُم بِٱلْبَيِّنَـٰتِ فَرَدُّوٓا۟ أَيْدِيَهُمْ فِىٓ أَفْوَٰهِهِمْ وَقَالُوٓا۟ إِنَّا كَفَرْنَا بِمَآ أُرْسِلْتُم بِهِۦ وَإِنَّا لَفِى شَكٍّ مِّمَّا تَدْعُونَنَآ إِلَيْهِ مُرِيبٍ ﴿٩﴾ ﴾

Stop Sounds

 Study

While symbols are helpful in showing you where to stop or continue, they do not explain what a break in recitation actually sounds like. Listen and repeat the verses below taking care to note the sounds at the points of stopping.

Group 1

﴿ وَيَمْنَعُونَ ٱلْمَاعُونَ ۝ ﴾

﴿ وَمَن يَعْمَلْ مِثْقَالَ ذَرَّةٍ شَرًّا يَرَهُ ۝ ﴾

﴿ وَهَٰذَا ٱلْبَلَدِ ٱلْأَمِينِ ۝ ﴾

Group 2

﴿ كِتَٰبٌ مَّرْقُومٌ ۝ ﴾

﴿ سَيَصْلَىٰ نَارًا ذَاتَ لَهَبٍ ۝ ﴾

Group 3

﴿ فَسَوْفَ يُحَاسَبُ حِسَابًا يَسِيرًا ۝ ﴾

﴿ وَأَنَّهُ تَعَٰلَىٰ جَدُّ رَبِّنَا مَا ٱتَّخَذَ صَٰحِبَةً وَلَا وَلَدًا ۝ ﴾

Group 4

﴿ تَصْلَىٰ نَارًا حَامِيَةً ۝ ﴾

﴿ وَزَرَابِيُّ مَبْثُوثَةٌ ۝ ﴾

﴿ وَفَٰكِهَةٍ كَثِيرَةٍ ۝ ﴾

You may have noticed that the sounds of letters with their *harakāt* (ﹷ ﹻ ﹹ ﹺ ﹲ) change when they occur at the point of a stop.

In Group 1, the short vowels (ﹷ ﹻ ﹹ) were removed when pronouncing the last letter of the word and were replaced with a *sukoon* (ﹿ). For example the word (ٱلْأَمِينِ) is pronounced as (ٱلْأَمِينْ).

The same rule applies to Group 2 in which all the words end in either *dhummatayn* (ﹹ) or *kasratayn* (ﹺ).

In Group 3, the last words all end in *fatḥatayn* (ﹶ). Here, the last letter is pronounced as if it has a *fatḥah* (ﹷ) and the letter *alif* (ا) after it. For example, the word (يَسِيرًا) is pronounced as (يَسِيرَا) and the word (وَلَدًا) is pronounced as (وَلَدَا).

In Group 4, all the last words end in a *tā marbūtah* (ة). No matter which *harakah* this letter has above it, the *harakah* sounds are removed and the *tā marbūtah* is pronounced as the letter *hā sākin* (ه). For example, the word (حَامِيَةٌ) is pronounced as (حَامِيَه).

Note

Note that this rule applies to tā marbūtah (ة) only and not to tā mabṣūtah (ت) which is pronounced according to the rule of Group 1.

Rule

When stopping on a word, the last letter has its *harakāt* (ﹷ ﹻ ﹹ ﹺ ﹲ) replaced with *sukoon* (ﹿ) and is pronounced accordingly. The only exception to this rule is when the last letter ends in a *fatḥatayn* (ﹶ) in which case it is pronounced as if one of the *fatḥah* (ﹷ) has been removed and the letter *alif* has been added after the last letter.

If the last word ends in a *tā marbūtah* (ة), it is pronounced as if the *tā marbūtah* (ة) is removed along with its *harakah* and replaced with the letter *hā sākin* (ه).

Rewrite the following words as you would pronounce them if they were at the point of a pause or stop.

Written	Pronounced
ٱلْمُتَّقُونَ	
كَاذِبَةٌ	
عَجِيبٌ	
عَسِيرٌ	
عَشِرٍ	
ٱلرَّحِيمِ	
أَحَدُ	
تُرْجَعُونَ	
كُبَّارًا	
وَيَسَرَ	
ذِكْرًا	
مُرِيبٍ	

Practice

Recite the following verses taking care to stop or continue at the appropriate places and to pronounce the last word at the point of any stop correctly.

Line 1

﴿ إِنَّا هَدَيْنَٰهُ ٱلسَّبِيلَ إِمَّا شَاكِرًا وَإِمَّا كَفُورًا ۞ ﴾

Line 2

﴿ وَلَقَدْ يَسَّرْنَا ٱلْقُرْءَانَ لِلذِّكْرِ فَهَلْ مِن مُّدَّكِرٍ ۞ ﴾

Line 3

﴿ قَالَ يَٰقَوْمِ إِنِّي لَكُمْ نَذِيرٌ مُّبِينٌ ۞ ﴾

Line 4

﴿ أَوْ مِسْكِينًا ذَا مَتْرَبَةٍ ۞ ﴾

Line 5

﴿ رَسُولٌ مِّنَ ٱللَّهِ يَتْلُوا۟ صُحُفًا مُّطَهَّرَةً ۞ ﴾

Line 6

﴿ ضَاحِكَةٌ مُّسْتَبْشِرَةٌ ۞ ﴾

Line 7

﴿ وَجَعَلْنَا ٱلَّيْلَ لِبَاسًا ۞ ﴾

Line 8

﴿ وَهُوَ ٱلْغَفُورُ ٱلْوَدُودُ ۞ ﴾

Line 9

﴿ وَقَالُوا۟ لَوْ كُنَّا نَسْمَعُ أَوْ نَعْقِلُ مَا كُنَّا فِىٓ أَصْحَٰبِ ٱلسَّعِيرِ ۞ ﴾

Line 10

﴿ فَأَصْحَٰبُ ٱلْمَيْمَنَةِ مَآ أَصْحَٰبُ ٱلْمَيْمَنَةِ ۞ ﴾

س Pause

Study

Listen and repeat each of the following verses:

Example 1

﴿ وَقِيلَ مَنْۜ رَاقٍ ﴿٢٧﴾ ﴾

Example 2

﴿ قَالُواْ يَٰوَيۡلَنَا مَنۢ بَعَثَنَا مِن مَّرۡقَدِنَاۜۗ هَٰذَا مَا وَعَدَ ٱلرَّحۡمَٰنُ
وَصَدَقَ ٱلۡمُرۡسَلُونَ ﴿٥٢﴾ ﴾

Reflect

Harakah Measure
The notion of a count or ***harakah*** *will recur in later chapters. Refer to the Glossary on page 72 for a quick reminder of the definition.*

You may have noticed that in each verse there was a pause in the recitation at the point where the symbol (س) occurred. Unlike the 'stop' covered in the previous chapter, a pause is achieved by stopping the recitation whilst holding your breath. The duration of this hold is for two counts or ***harakāt*** (حَرَكَات), and is measured by the time it would take to say a long vowel such as '*aa*' (تَا), '*ee*' (تِي) or '*oo*' (تُو).

Pause Examples
The pause rule only occurs on five occasions in the Noble Quran. Two have been mentioned in the examples above, and the remaining three are included in the practice section that follows.

Rule

The symbol (س) means you must pause in your recitation by holding your breath for two counts.

Practice

Read the following verses, taking care to observe the pause correctly.

﴿ كَلَّاۖ بَلْۜ رَانَ عَلَىٰ قُلُوبِهِم مَّا كَانُواْ يَكْسِبُونَ ﴿١٤﴾ ﴾

Line 1

﴿ مَآ أَغْنَىٰ عَنِّي مَالِيَهْۜ ﴿٢٨﴾ هَلَكَ عَنِّي سُلْطَٰنِيَهْ ﴿٢٩﴾ ﴾

Line 2

﴿ ٱلْحَمْدُ لِلَّهِ ٱلَّذِيٓ أَنزَلَ عَلَىٰ عَبْدِهِ ٱلْكِتَٰبَ وَلَمْ يَجْعَل لَّهُۥ عِوَجَاۜ

﴿١﴾ قَيِّمًا لِّيُنذِرَ بَأْسًا شَدِيدًا مِّن لَّدُنْهُ وَيُبَشِّرَ ٱلْمُؤْمِنِينَ ٱلَّذِينَ

يَعْمَلُونَ ٱلصَّٰلِحَٰتِ أَنَّ لَهُمْ أَجْرًا حَسَنًا ﴿٢﴾ ﴾

Line 3

Rule

The pause symbol (ۜ) we have just studied always occurs between two words. However a similar symbol is also used for another purpose in the Quran. It occurs within a word and only on the letter *ṣād* (ص). In this instance the letter *ṣād* (ص) is pronounced as a *seen* (س). There are only three occasions where it occurs in the Quran:

Reference	Word	Ruling
Al-Baqarah: 245	وَيَبْصُۜطُ	*Ṣād* (ص) must be pronounced as a *seen* (س)
Al-A'rāf: 69	بَصْۜطَةً	*Ṣād* (ص) must be pronounced as a *seen* (س)
At-Tur: 37	ٱلْمُصَۣيْطِرُونَ	*Ṣād* (ص) may be pronounced as a *seen* (س) or a *ṣād* (ص)

Symbol Placement

Note that in the instances where the pronounciation is compulsory, the seen symbol (ۜ) is shown above the letter ṣād (ص). In the last instance where the seen (س) pronounciation is optional, the seen symbol (ۜ) occurs below the letter ṣād (ص).

Study

Listen and repeat each of the following letters:

Group 1

ظ	ط	ض	ص
	غ	خ	ق

Group 2

ث	ت	ب	ء
ذ	د	ح	ج
ع	ش	س	ز
ن	م	ك	ف
	ي	ه	و

Reflect

Memory Tip

These letters can be summarised through the words:

(خُصَّ ضَغْطٍ قِظْ)

You may have noticed that the letters in Group 1 have a much heavier sound when compared to the letters in Group 2. This heavy sound is referred to as *tafkheem* (تَفْخِيم). The letters of Group 1 are:

ظ ق ط ض ص خ

These are known as the letters of 'elevation' or *isti'lā* (الاستعلاء). Elevation is a characteristic of these letters where the tongue is raised to the rear roof of the mouth when the letter is pronounced. The letters that have the heaviest sounds from among these seven are:

ظ ط ض ص

These four letters carry an additional characteristic of a puckering of the mouth when they are pronounced, referred to as *al-itbāq* (الاطباق).

In contrast, the rest of the letters in the alphabet (see Group 2), all have a light sound referred to as *tarqeeq* (تَرْقِيق). They carry the opposite characteristic of 'elevation' and are known as the letters of 'lowness' or *istinfāl* (الاستنفال). They are pronounced with the tongue generally in a lowered position away from the rear-roof of the mouth.

Task

Which two letters have not been mentioned in this chapter as either letters of *tafkheem* or *tarqeeq*?

....

Rule

The letters that are pronounced with a heavy sound are known as letters of *tafkheem*. They are:

ظ ق ط ض ص غ خ

All the letters of *tafkheem* have the characteristic of 'elevation' of the tongue. The heaviest of the *tafkheem* letters are those which carry an additional characteristic of a 'puckering' of the mouth. They are:

ظ ط ض ص

The letters pronounced with a light sound are known as letters of *tarqeeq*. They are the remaining letters of the alphabet (with the exception of ل and ر) and they all have the characteristic of 'lowness' of the tongue during pronunciation.

Complete the table to categorise the letters of *tafkheem* and *tarqeeq*. In the *tafkheem* category, circle the lightest letters in the group.

Letters of Tafkheem	Letters of Tarqeeq

Practice

Recite the verses below taking care to pronounce the letters of *tafkheem* and *tarqeeq* correctly.

Line 1

﴿ إِلَّا ٱلَّذِينَ ءَامَنُواْ وَعَمِلُواْ ٱلصَّـٰلِحَـٰتِ فَلَهُمْ أَجْرٌ غَيْرُ مَمْنُونٍ ۝ ﴾

Line 2

﴿ قُلْ أَرَءَيْتُمْ إِنْ أَصْبَحَ مَاؤُكُمْ غَوْرًا فَمَن يَأْتِيكُم بِمَآءٍ مَّعِينٍ ۝ ﴾

Line 3

﴿ فَرَاغَ عَلَيْهِمْ ضَرْبًا بِٱلْيَمِينِ ۝ ﴾

Line 4

﴿ قَالَ أَتَعْبُدُونَ مَا تَنْحِتُونَ ۝ ﴾

Line 5

﴿ وَٱصْبِرْ عَلَىٰ مَا يَقُولُونَ وَٱهْجُرْهُمْ هَجْرًا جَمِيلًا ﴿١٠﴾ ﴾

Line 6

﴿ وَأَمَّا مَنْ خَافَ مَقَامَ رَبِّهِۦ وَنَهَى ٱلنَّفْسَ عَنِ ٱلْهَوَىٰ ﴿٤٠﴾ ﴾

Line 7

﴿ وَمَا تَشَآءُونَ إِلَّآ أَن يَشَآءَ ٱللَّهُ رَبُّ ٱلْعَٰلَمِينَ ﴿٢٩﴾ ﴾

Line 8

﴿ فَٱلْيَوْمَ ٱلَّذِينَ ءَامَنُوا۟ مِنَ ٱلْكُفَّارِ يَضْحَكُونَ ﴿٣٤﴾ ﴾

Line 9

﴿ هَلْ أَتَىٰ عَلَى ٱلْإِنسَٰنِ حِينٌ مِّنَ ٱلدَّهْرِ لَمْ يَكُن شَيْـًٔا مَّذْكُورًا ﴿١﴾ ﴾

Line 10

﴿ وَمَا تَشَآءُونَ إِلَّآ أَن يَشَآءَ ٱللَّهُ رَبُّ ٱلْعَٰلَمِينَ ﴿٢٩﴾ ﴾

Line 11

﴿ وَأَمَّآ إِذَا مَا ٱبْتَلَىٰهُ فَقَدَرَ عَلَيْهِ رِزْقَهُۥ فَيَقُولُ رَبِّىٓ أَهَٰنَنِ ﴿١٦﴾ ﴾

Line 12

﴿ وَقَالُوا۟ لَوْ كُنَّا نَسْمَعُ أَوْ نَعْقِلُ مَا كُنَّا فِىٓ أَصْحَٰبِ ٱلسَّعِيرِ ﴿١٠﴾ ﴾

Line 13

﴿ إِذَا تُتْلَىٰ عَلَيْهِ ءَايَٰتُنَا قَالَ أَسَٰطِيرُ ٱلْأَوَّلِينَ ﴿١٥﴾ ﴾

Line 14

﴿ وَأَمَّا عَادٌ فَأُهْلِكُوا۟ بِرِيحٍ صَرْصَرٍ عَاتِيَةٍ ﴿٦﴾ ﴾

Line 15

﴿ يَهْدِىٓ إِلَى ٱلرُّشْدِ فَـَٔامَنَّا بِهِۦ ۖ وَلَن نُّشْرِكَ بِرَبِّنَآ أَحَدًا ﴿٢﴾ ﴾

Line 16

﴿ وَجَعَلَ ٱلْقَمَرَ فِيهِنَّ نُورًا وَجَعَلَ ٱلشَّمْسَ سِرَاجًا ﴿١٦﴾ ﴾

Laam Rules

Listen and repeat each of the following words:

Group 1

لَكُم	لَا	ٱلَّذِينَ
أَلِيمٍ	وَلِلرَّسُولِ	أَهْلِ
ٱلرَّسُولُ	ٱقْتَتَلُواْ	فَقَـٰتِلُواْ
فَبِإِذْنِ ٱللَّه	فَلِلَّه	فَبِإِذْنِ ٱللَّه

Group 2

إِلَى ٱللَّه	إِنَّ ٱللَّهَ	أَفَآءَ ٱللَّهُ
ءَاتَىٰهُ ٱللَّهُ	فَوَقَىٰهُمُ ٱللَّهُ	وَٱتَّقُوا۟ ٱللَّهَ

Reflect

You may have noticed that the pronounciation of *lām* (ل) differs in the two groups. In Group 1, (ل) is pronounced with *tarqeeq*, while in Group 2 it is pronounced with *tafkheem*.

The letter (ل) is normally pronounced with *tarqeeq*. The only exception to this rule is when (ل) occurs in the divine name 'Allah' (الله), and the last letter of the word before it ends in a *fatḥah* (ﹷ) or *dhummah* (ﹹ). In this case, the letter (ل) is pronounced with *tafkheem*, as seen in the examples in Group 2.

Rule

The letter *lām* (ل) is normally pronounced with *tarqeeq*. The only exception to this rule is when *lām* (ل) occurs in the divine name *Allah* (الله), and the last letter of the word before it ends in a *fathah* (◌َ) or *dhummah* (◌ُ). In this case, the letter *lām* (ل) is pronounced with *tafkheem*.

Task

Search the Quran for some examples of (ل) *tafkheem* and (ل) *tarqeeq* and categorise them in the table below.

Tafkheem	Tarqeeq

Practice

Read the verse below taking care to pronounce the (ل) of *tafkheem* and (ل) of *tarqeeq* correctly.

﴿ ذَٰلِكَ بِأَنَّهُمْ شَآقُّوا۟ ٱللَّهَ وَرَسُولَهُۥ ۚ وَمَن يُشَاقِّ ٱللَّهَ فَإِنَّ ٱللَّهَ شَدِيدُ ٱلْعِقَابِ ﴾

Raa Rules

Study

Listen and repeat each of the following words:

Group 1

فَارِقُوهُنَّ	كَرِيمٍ	يُرِيدُ

Group 2

وَٱسْتَغْفِرْ	يَغْفِرْ	فِرْعَوْنَ

Group 3

ٱلْمَصِيرُ	حَسِيرٌ	نَذِيرٌ

Group 4

وَبِئْرٍ	قِطْرًا	حِجْرٍ

Group 5

فَٱرْجِعِ	مَعْرُوفٍ	ٱلْبَصَرَ
خُسْرٍ	قُرْءَانٌ	تَفُورُ
وَٱلْعَصْرِ	مَنِ ٱرْتَضَىٰ	مِرْصَادًا

Reflect

You may have noticed that the letter *rā* (ر) is pronounced differently in each group. The (ر) contained in the words in Groups 1-4 was pronounced with *tarqeeq*, while in the words in Group 5, it was pronounced with *tafkheem*.

(ر) was pronounced lightly with *tarqeeq* because of the following reasons:

- **Group 1:** The letter *rā* itself carries a *kasrah* (رِ).

- **Group 2:** The letter *rā* carries a *sukoon* (رْ) and the letter before it carries a *kasrah* (ـِ).

- **Group 3:** If you stop on the letter (ر) during recitation and the letter before it is a *yā* carrying a *sukoon* (يْ).

- **Group 4:** If you stop on the letter (ر) during recitation and the letter before it carries a *sukoon* (ـْ) and the letter before that carries a *kasrah* (ـِ).

In all other cases, (ر) is pronounced with *tafkheem* as shown by the examples in Group 5.

Rule

The letter (ر) is pronounced with *tafkheem* except in the following cases where it is pronounced with *tarqeeq*:

- The letter *rā* carries a *kasrah* (رِ).

- The letter *rā* carries a *sukoon* (رْ) and the letter before it carries a *kasrah* (ـِ).

- If you stop on (ر) and the letter before it is a *yā* carrying a *sukoon* (يْ).

- If you stop on (ر) and the letter before it carries a *sukoon* (ـْ) and the letter before that carries a *kasrah* (ـِ).

Task

Search the Quran for examples of (ر) *tafkheem* and (ر) *tarqeeq* and categorise them in the table below.

Tafkheem	Tarqeeq

Practice

Recite the verses below taking care to pronounce the (ر) of *tafkheem* and the (ر) of *tarqeeq* correctly.

﴿ وَإِن يَكَادُ ٱلَّذِينَ كَفَرُواْ لَيُزْلِقُونَكَ بِأَبْصَـٰرِهِمْ لَمَّا سَمِعُواْ ٱلذِّكْرَ

Line 1

وَيَقُولُونَ إِنَّهُۥ لَمَجْنُونٌ ﴿۵۱﴾ ﴾

﴿ قُلْ أُوحِيَ إِلَىَّ أَنَّهُ ٱسْتَمَعَ نَفَرٌ مِّنَ ٱلْجِنِّ فَقَالُوٓاْ إِنَّا سَمِعْنَا قُرْءَانًا

Line 2

عَجَبًا ﴿۱﴾ ﴾

﴿ وَٱلْمُرْسَلَٰتِ عُرْفًا ۝ ﴾

Line 3

﴿ يَٰٓأَيُّهَا ٱلْإِنسَٰنُ مَا غَرَّكَ بِرَبِّكَ ٱلْكَرِيمِ ۝ ﴾

Line 4

﴿ وَأَمَّآ إِذَا مَا ٱبْتَلَىٰهُ فَقَدَرَ عَلَيْهِ رِزْقَهُۥ فَيَقُولُ رَبِّىٓ أَهَٰنَنِ ۝ ﴾

Line 5

﴿ قُلْ أَرَءَيْتُمْ إِنْ أَصْبَحَ مَآؤُكُمْ غَوْرًا فَمَن يَأْتِيكُم بِمَآءٍ مَّعِينٍ ۝ ﴾

Line 6

﴿ فَٱعْتَرَفُوا۟ بِذَنۢبِهِمْ فَسُحْقًا لِّأَصْحَٰبِ ٱلسَّعِيرِ ۝ ﴾

Line 7

﴿ قَوَارِيرَا۟ مِن فِضَّةٍ قَدَّرُوهَا تَقْدِيرًا ۝ ﴾

Line 8

﴿ وَلِرَبِّكَ فَٱصْبِرْ ۝ ﴾

Line 9

﴿ وَمَكَرُوا۟ مَكْرًا كُبَّارًا ۝ ﴾

Line 10

﴿ وَٱصْبِرْ عَلَىٰ مَا يَقُولُونَ وَٱهْجُرْهُمْ هَجْرًا جَمِيلًا ۝ ﴾

Line 11

﴿ إِنَّ ٱلَّذِينَ كَفَرُوا۟ مِنْ أَهْلِ ٱلْكِتَٰبِ وَٱلْمُشْرِكِينَ فِى نَارِ جَهَنَّمَ خَٰلِدِينَ فِيهَآ أُو۟لَٰٓئِكَ هُمْ شَرُّ ٱلْبَرِيَّةِ ۝ ﴾

Line 12

﴿ إِنَّآ أَرْسَلْنَآ إِلَيْكُمْ رَسُولًا شَٰهِدًا عَلَيْكُمْ كَمَآ أَرْسَلْنَآ إِلَىٰ فِرْعَوْنَ رَسُولًا ۝ ﴾

Line 13

Qalqalah

Listen and repeat each of the following words:

Group 1

تَقْوَٰهُمْ   وَيُدْخِلُهُمْ   لِيَجْزِىَ   قَبْلِهِمْ   أَطْعَمَهُمْ

Group 2

ٱلْفَلَقِ   يُولَدْ   مَّرِيجٍ   ٱلْحَطَبِ   مُحِيطٌ

Group 3

ٱلْحَقُّ   مَدَّ   حَجَّ   وَتَبَّ

Reflect

Memory Tip

The letters of qalqalah are summarised by the sentence:
(قُطْبُ جَدٍّ)

You may have noticed that in Group 1, every word contains a letter in the middle carrying a *sukoon* (ـْ) and that a faint echo sound was produced when the letter was pronounced. The letters on which this echo could be heard were:

د   ج   ب   ط   ق

In Group 2, you may have noticed that the same set of letters occur at the end of the words and so they were pronounced with a *sukoon* (ـْ). You may have noticed that while the echo could still be heard, it was a little stronger in comparison to the case in Group 1.

In Group 3, the letters occur at the end of the words and also carry a *shaddah* (ّ). You may have noticed that the echo sound was the strongest of all in Group 3 when compared to the other two groups.

The echo sound is called *qalqalah* (قلقلة) and is not strong enough to reach the level of a *fatḥah* (ـَ). Qalqalah is a characteristic of the letters mentioned above, and without it, the sound of the letters would not be clearly known during recitation.

Task

Try to pronounce the words in the groups with and without the *qalqalah*. Which of the two recitations feels more natural to you? Which of the two recitations leads to a clearer sound of the letters?

Rule

Whenever the letters:

ق ط ب ج د

carry (or are pronounced as if they carry) a *sukoon*, they are pronounced with an echo sound known as *qalqalah*. The duration of the echo sound is shorter than that of a *fatḥah* (ـَ). The strength of the *qalqalah* varies and is weakest when it occurs in the middle of a word, stronger when it occurs at the end of a word, and strongest when it occurs at the end of a word while carrying a *shaddah* (ّ).

Task

Search the Quran for examples of *qalqalah* and categorise them in the table that follows in accordance to their strength.

Weak	Medium	Strong

Recite the verses below taking care to pronounce the *qalqalah* correctly.

Line 1

﴿ تَبْصِرَةً وَذِكْرَىٰ لِكُلِّ عَبْدٍ مُّنِيبٍ ۝ ﴾

Line 2

﴿ رِّزْقًا لِّلْعِبَادِ ۖ وَأَحْيَيْنَا بِهِۦ بَلْدَةً مَّيْتًا ۚ كَذَٰلِكَ ٱلْخُرُوجُ ۝ ﴾

Line 3

﴿ وَعَادٌ وَفِرْعَوْنُ وَإِخْوَانُ لُوطٍ ۝ ﴾

Line 4

﴿ كَذَّبَتْ قَبْلَهُمْ قَوْمُ نُوحٍ وَأَصْحَابُ ٱلرَّسِّ وَثَمُودُ ۝ ﴾

Line 5

﴿ يَوْمَ نَبْطِشُ ٱلْبَطْشَةَ ٱلْكُبْرَىٰ إِنَّا مُنتَقِمُونَ ۝ ﴾

Line 6

﴿ ذُقْ إِنَّكَ أَنتَ ٱلْعَزِيزُ ٱلْكَرِيمُ ۝ ﴾

Line 7

﴿ تَبَّتْ يَدَآ أَبِى لَهَبٍ وَتَبَّ ۝ ﴾

Line 8

﴿ وَٱلسَّمَآءِ وَٱلطَّارِقِ ۝ ﴾

Ghunnah

In the chapter of *makhārij-ul huroof* (مخارج الحروف) on page 8, we mentioned that from the *makhraj* of the nasal passage emerges a sound called *ghunnah* (غنّة). In this chapter, we shall explore this sound and the instances in which it appears.

Study

Listen and repeat each of the following words:

Group 1

ٱلنَّهَارَ	كَأَنَّهُۥ	إِنَّهَا
وَٱلنَّشِطَتِ	وَٱلنَّزِعَتِ	وَجَنَّتٍ
ٱلنَّاسِ	ٱلنَّجْدَينِ	ٱلنُّجُومُ

Group 2

نَفْسٌ مَّا	ثَمَّ	وَأَمَّا
فَأُمُّهُۥ	قُرْءَانٌ مَّجِيدٌ	ثُمَّ
أَكْلًا لَّمًّا	عَمَدٍ مُّمَدَّدَةٍ	عَلَيْهِم مُّؤْصَدَةٌ

Reflect

You may have noticed that each of the examples in Group 1 contain the letter *noon* with a *shaddah* (نّ) and that each of the examples in Group 2 contain the letter *meem* with a *shaddah* (مّ). You may also have noticed that both these letters were pronounced with a nasal sound that was held for the duration of two *harakāt*. In the case of the letter *noon* (ن), the *ghunnah* is produced by blocking the flow of sound using the tongue, while in the case of the letter *meem* (م), it is produced by blocking the flow of sound using the lips.

Rule

The letter *noon* with a *shaddah* (نّ) and the letter *meem* with a *shaddah* (مّ) are pronounced with a nasal sound known as *ghunnah*. The *ghunnah* sound is held for a duration of two *harakāt*.

Task

Search the Quran for examples of *ghunnah* and categorise them in the table below.

Noon Shaddah	Meem Shaddah

Practice

Recite the verses below taking care to pronounce the *ghunnah* correctly.

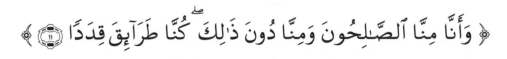

Line 1 ﴿ وَأَنَّا مِنَّا ٱلصَّـٰلِحُونَ وَمِنَّا دُونَ ذَٰلِكَ ۖ كُنَّا طَرَآئِقَ قِدَدًا ﴿١١﴾ ﴾

Line 2 ﴿ وَٱلَّذِينَ هُم مِّنْ عَذَابِ رَبِّهِم مُّشْفِقُونَ ﴿٢٧﴾ ﴾

Noon Saakin & Tanween

Study

Listen and repeat each of the following words:

Group 1

مِّنْ عِندِنَا	وَمِنْهُمْ	عَذَابًا أَلِيمًا
مَّنْ خَشِىَ	قَوْمًا غَيْرَكُمْ	عَلِيمًا حَكِيمًا

Group 2

بِقَلْبٍ مُّنِيبٍ	مِن رَّبِّهِمْ	وَمَن يُطِعِ
مَّن نَّشَاءُ	حَرَجٌ وَلَا	مَن لَّعَنَهُ

Group 3

أَنبِئْهُم	عَنْ بَعْضٍ	مِّنْ بَيْنِنَآ

Group 4

بَعُوضَةً فَمَا	لِتُنفِقُواْ	جَنَّتٍ تَجْرِى

Reflect

Quick Question

Why do you think noon saakin & tanween are treated in the same way, even though they do not appear or look the same?

You may have noticed that all the words in the groups above contain letters that are either:

- *noon* with a *sukoon* (نْ) (referred to as *noon sākin*) or
- any other letter carrying a *tanween* (ـً ـٍ ـٌ).

The rules for both these types of letters are the same, and we shall refer to both of these cases as *noon sākin & tanween* in the explanations that follow.

In Group 1 you may have noticed that both the *noon sākin & tanween* and the letter after it are pronounced clearly as normal. This clear pronounciation is called *ith-hār* (إظهار). You may also have noticed that the letters that come after the *noon sākin & tanween* are all letters of the throat:

خ غ ح ع ه ء

In Group 2, you may have noticed that the *noon sākin & tanween* only occurs at the end of the word (unlike in the other groups) and is merged into the first letter of the word after it. This type of merging is called *idghām* (إدغام) and occurs when *noon sākin & tanween* is followed by one of the following letters:

ي ر م ل و ن

The *idghām* is pronounced with *ghunnah* with all these letter except *lām* (ل) and *rā* (ر). You may have noticed that *idghām* with *noon sākin & tanween* only occurs between two words.

In Group 3, the *noon sākin & tanween* is followed by the letter *bā* (ب). In this case, the *noon sākin & tanween* turns into the letter *meem* (م). This change is called *iqlāb* (الإقلاب). This *meem* (م) is then pronounced with a hiding sound known as *ikhfā* (الإخفاء - see below) and is discussed in more detail in the next chapter.

In Group 4, you may have noticed that the *noon sākin & tanween* is pronounced as if it is being concealed or hiding behind the letter after it. This concealment is called *ikhfā* (الإخفاء) and sounds like something in between *ith-hār* and *idghām* whilst still being pronounced with *ghunnah*. *Ikhfā* occurs when *noon sākin & tanween* is followed by the remaining letters of the alphabet, namely:

ز ذ د ج ث ت ك ق ف

ظ ط ض ص ش س

Note

Ith-hār can occur in a single word as in the case of noon sākin or between two words as in the case of tanween.

Memory Tip

The letters of idghām with noon saakin & tanween are summarised by the word (يَرْمَلُونْ). Taking the letters (ل) and (ر) out of this word, we get (يَنْمُوْ).

53

Rule

Noon *sākin & tanween* are pronounced in one of the following four ways depending on the letters that follow them:

Ruling	Comment	Following Letters		
Ith-hār	Noon *sākin & tanween* are pronounced clearly without *ghunnah*.	ع	ه	ء
		خ	غ	ح
Idghām	Noon *sākin & tanween* merge with the letter after it. This occurs with *ghunnah*, except for the letters *lām* (ل) and *rā* (ر). *Idghām* only occurs with *noon sākin* and *tanween* coming at the end of a word and merging with the first letter of the word that follows.	م	ر	ي
		ن	و	ل
Iqlāb	Noon *sākin & tanween* turns in to the letter *meem* (م) and is pronounced with *ikhfā*.	ب		
Ikhfā	Noon *sākin & tanween* are pronounced as if they are hiding behind the letter after them.	د	ذ	ز
		ت	ث	ج
		ف	ق	ك
		ض	ط	ظ
		س	ش	ص

Task

Search the Quran for examples of *noon sākin & tanween* and categorise them in the table below.

Ith-haar	Idghaam	Iqlaab	Ikhfaa

Practice

Recite the verses below taking care to pronounce *noon sākin & tanween* correctly.

﴿ وَكَذَٰلِكَ فَتَنَّا بَعْضَهُم بِبَعْضٍ لِّيَقُولُوٓاْ أَهَٰٓؤُلَآءِ مَنَّ ٱللَّهُ

عَلَيْهِم مِّنۢ بَيْنِنَآ أَلَيْسَ ٱللَّهُ بِأَعْلَمَ بِٱلشَّـٰكِرِينَ ۝ ﴾

Line 1

﴿ وَإِذَا رَأَيْتَ ثَمَّ رَأَيْتَ نَعِيمًا وَمُلْكًا كَبِيرًا ۝ ﴾

Line 2

﴿ مَّنْ خَشِيَ ٱلرَّحْمَٰنَ بِٱلْغَيْبِ وَجَآءَ بِقَلْبٍ مُّنِيبٍ ۝ ﴾

Line 3

﴿ نِّعْمَةً مِّنْ عِندِنَا ۚ كَذَٰلِكَ نَجْزِى مَن شَكَرَ ۝ ﴾

Line 4

Study

Listen and repeat each of the following words:

Group 1

نَبِّهِم مِّن   هُم مِّن   رَبِّهِم مُّشْفِقُونَ

Group 2

عَلِيمٌ بِذَاتِ   مِنْ بَعْدِ   بَعْضَهُم بِبَعْضٍ

Group 3

بِأَنَّهُمْ قَالُواْ   دُمْتَ   أَلَمْ أَقُل

Reflect

You may have noticed that all the words in the groups contain the letter *meem* with a *sukoon* (مْ) referred to as *meem sākin*.

In Group 1, *meem sākin* is followed by another *meem* and is merged into it. This type of merging is called *idghām* of the lips or *idghām ash-shafawi* (الإدغام الشفوي). A *shaddah* (ـّـ) is added to the second *meem* to indicate the *idghām*, and it is pronounced with *ghunnah*.

In Group 2, you may have noticed that the *meem sākin* is followed by the letter *bā* (ب). When pronounced together, they sound as if the *meem* is hiding behind the *bā*. This is known as *ikhfā ash-shafawi* (الإخفاء الشفوي) and is pronounced with *ghunnah*.

In Group 3, the *meem sākin* is followed by letters other than *meem* or *bā*. In this case the *meem sākin* is pronounced clearly without *ghunnah*. This clear pronounciation is called *ith-hār ash-shafawi* (الإظهار الشفوي).

Rule

When the letter *meem* appears with a *sukoon* (مْ), it is pronounced as follows:

Letter Before (مْ)	Pronounciation
Meem (م)	Idghām Ash-Shafawi
Bā (ب)	Ikhfā Ash-Shafawi
All other letters	Ith-hār Ash-Shafawi

Task

Search the Quran for examples of *meem sākin* and categorise them in the table below.

Idghaam	Ikhfaa	Ith-haar

Practice

Recite the verses below taking care to pronounce *meem sākin* correctly.

﴾ فَهَلْ تَرَىٰ لَهُم مِّنۢ بَاقِيَةٍ ۝ ﴿

Line 1

﴾ وَأَنَّا لَمَّا سَمِعْنَا ٱلْهُدَىٰٓ ءَامَنَّا بِهِۦ ۖ فَمَن يُؤْمِنۢ بِرَبِّهِۦ فَلَا يَخَافُ بَخْسًا وَلَا رَهَقًا ۝ ﴿

Line 2

Idghaam

Idghām does not only occur with *noon sākin*, *meem sākin* and *tanween*. We will now take a look at some other instances where the merging of two letters occurs.

Study

Listen and repeat each of the following words:

Group 1

يُدْرِككُّمۡ   يُسۡرِف فِّى   ٱضۡرِب بِّعَصَاكَ

Group 2

أُجِيبَت دَّعۡوَتُكُمَا   بَسَطتَ   إذ ظَّلَمۡتُمۡ

فَـَٔامَنَت طَّآئِفَةٌ   ٱرۡكَب مَّعَنَا   يَلۡهَث ذَّٰلِكَ

Group 3

نَخۡلُقكُّمۡ   وَقُل رَّبِّ

Reflect

You may have noticed that in Group 1 every example has a letter that occurs twice consecutively. In the first example, the letter *bā* (ب) appears at the end of the first word and at the beginning of the second word. The letter need not repeat consecutively across two seperate words, but rather it can repeat itself consecutively in one word, as in the third example.

In any case, when this type of repetition occurs and the first letter carries a *sukoon* (ـْ), the two letters merge into one another. This is indicated by a *shaddah* (ـّ) on the second letter and is referred to as *idghām al-mutamāthilayn* (الإدغام المتماثلين). In the case where this occurs with the letters *meem* (م) or *noon* (ن), a *ghunnah* sound is observed.

In Group 2, you may have noticed that the merging letters in each example are from the same *makhraj* but have different *sifāt*, such as the letters (ط) and (ت) in the second example. This *idghām* of similar letters is called *idghām al-mutajānisayn* (الإدغام المتجانسين). This occurs with the following letters:

- (ذ) followed by (ظ)
- (ت) followed by (د) or (ط)
- (د) followed by (ت)
- (ط) followed by (ت)
- (ب) followed by (م)
- (ث) followed by (ذ)

In Group 3, you would have noticed that the merging letters are:

- (ل) followed by *rā* (ر)
- (ق) followed by *kaaf* (ك)

These pairs do not have the same *makhraj*, but thier *makhārij* are close to each other. Merging of these letters of close proximity is called *idghām al-mutaqāribayn* (الإدغام المتقاربين).

Rule

Idghām of two consecutive letters occurs in the following three cases:

Type	Comments	Letters
Mutamāthilayn	If the same letter appears consecutively and the first of them is carrying a *sukoon* (ـْ). In the case where this occurs with the letters *meem* (م) or *noon* (ن), a *ghunnah* sound is observed.	Any letter followed by itself.

Continued...

Mutajānisayn	When two consecutive letters have the same *makhraj*.	• (ذ) followed by (ظ) • (ت) followed by (د) or (ط) • (د) followed by (ت) • (ط) followed by (ت) • (ب) followed by (م) • (ث) followed by (ذ)
Mutaqāribayn	When the two consecutive letters do not have the same *makhraj*, but their *makhārij* are close to each other.	• (ل) followed by (ر) • (ق) followed by (ك)

Task

Search the Quran for examples of *idghām* other than those of *noon sākin*, *tanween* and *meem sākin*. Categorise your results in the table below.

Same	Similar	Close Proximity

Practice ⟳

Recite the verses below taking care to pronounce *idghām* correctly.

﴿ وَإِذَا جَآءُوكُمْ قَالُوٓاْ ءَامَنَّا وَقَد دَّخَلُواْ بِٱلْكُفْرِ وَهُمْ قَدْ خَرَجُواْ بِهِۦ ۚ وَٱللَّهُ أَعْلَمُ بِمَا كَانُواْ يَكْتُمُونَ ﴿٦١﴾ ﴾

Line 1

﴿ ٱذْهَب بِّكِتَٰبِى هَٰذَا فَأَلْقِهْ إِلَيْهِمْ ثُمَّ تَوَلَّ عَنْهُمْ فَٱنظُرْ مَاذَا يَرْجِعُونَ ﴿٢٨﴾ ﴾

Line 2

﴿ بَل رَّفَعَهُ ٱللَّهُ إِلَيْهِ ۚ وَكَانَ ٱللَّهُ عَزِيزًا حَكِيمًا ﴿١٥٨﴾ ﴾

Line 3

﴿ وَلَوْلَآ أَن ثَبَّتْنَٰكَ لَقَدْ كِدتَّ تَرْكَنُ إِلَيْهِمْ شَيْئًا قَلِيلاً ﴿٧٤﴾ ﴾

Line 4

﴿ وَمَآ أَرْسَلْنَا مِن رَّسُولٍ إِلَّا لِيُطَاعَ بِإِذْنِ ٱللَّهِ ۚ وَلَوْ أَنَّهُمْ إِذ ظَّلَمُوٓاْ أَنفُسَهُمْ جَآءُوكَ فَٱسْتَغْفَرُواْ ٱللَّهَ وَٱسْتَغْفَرَ لَهُمُ ٱلرَّسُولُ لَوَجَدُواْ ٱللَّهَ تَوَّابًا رَّحِيمًا ﴿٦٤﴾ ﴾

Line 5

Rules of Hamza

The letter *hamza* is of two types:

- **Hamza Al-Qat'** (همزة القطع)**:** This is the standard letter from the Arabic alphabet indicated by the symbol (ء) and is pronounced with *ith-hār* in all cases.
- **Hamza Al-Wasl** (همزة الوصل)**:** This is a second type of *hamza* indicated by the symbol (ٱ) and has certain rulings related to it.

In this chapter, we will take a closer look at *hamza al-wasl*.

Study

Listen and repeat each of the following words:

—— Example 1 ——————————————————
ٱلنَّجْمُ

—— Example 2 ——————————————————
فَٱلْعَٰصِفَٰتِ

—— Example 3 ——————————————————
وَٱلسَّمَآءِ

—— Example 4 ——————————————————
وَٱلْمُرْسَلَٰتِ

In Example 1, you may have noticed that the *hamza al-wasl* occurs at the beginning of the word, and is pronounced with *ith-hār*. However in Example 2, it does not occur in the beginning of the word, and is not pronounced at all. Instead the recitation continues as if the *hamza* has been ommited completely.

When this ommision occurs in the case of the definite article *alif-lām* (ال) there are a further two different ways in which the recitation can proceed. If the letter following the definite article is from a category of letters called 'sun letters' (حروف الشمسية), *idghām* occurs and both the *hamza* and *lām* (ل) are completely ommited during recitation (see Example 3).

However, if the letter following the definite article is from a category of letters called the 'moon letters' (حروف القمرية), *ith-hār* occurs and the *sukoon* on the *lām* (ل) is pronoucned (see Example 4).

Accomplishing the task that follows will help you identify which letters are 'sun' letters and which of them are 'moon' letters.

Rule

Hamza al-wasl is pronounced with *ith-hār* if it occurs at the beginning of a word pronounced after a stop in recitation. If it does not occur at the beginning of a word, it is omitted completely.

When *hamza al-wasl* occurs in the definite article *alif-lām* (ال), it is pronounced in one of the following two ways:

* The *sukoon* on the *lām* is pronounced with *ith-hār* when followed by a moon letter.
* The *sukoon* on the *lām* is omitted when followed by a sun letter.

Task

For every letter of the Arabic alphabet, determine whether it is from the sun letters or moon letters.

Sun Letters	Moon Letters

Practice

Recite the verses below taking care to pronounce *hamza* correctly.

﴿ فَإِذَا جَاءَتِ ٱلطَّآمَّةُ ٱلْكُبْرَىٰ ۝ ﴾

Line 1

_____

﴿ ٱلَّذِى خَلَقَ فَسَوَّىٰ ۝ ﴾

Line 2

_____

﴿ وَٱذْكُرِ ٱسْمَ رَبِّكَ بُكْرَةً وَأَصِيلاً ۝ ﴾

Line 3

_____

﴿ كَلَّا وَٱلْقَمَرِ ۝ ﴾

Line 4

_____

﴿ وَٱلْتَفَّتِ ٱلسَّاقُ بِٱلسَّاقِ ۝ ﴾

Line 5

_____

﴿ وَٱلْجِبَالَ أَوْتَادًا ۝ ﴾

Line 6

_____

﴿ وَجَعَلَ ٱلْقَمَرَ فِيهِنَّ نُورًا وَجَعَلَ ٱلشَّمْسَ سِرَاجًا ۝ ﴾

Line 7

_____

﴿ وَأَلَّوِ ٱسْتَقَمُوا عَلَى ٱلطَّرِيقَةِ لَأَسْقَيْنَهُم مَّآءً غَدَقًا ۝ ﴾

Line 8

_____

﴿ أَيَحْسَبُ ٱلْإِنسَٰنُ أَن يُتْرَكَ سُدًى ۝ ﴾

Line 9

_____

Natural Madd

Study

Listen and repeat each of the following words:

Group 1

وَٱلظَّـٰلِمِينَ   يُوفِضُونَ   كَانَتْ

Group 2

ٱسْتِكْبَارًا   كَثِيرًا   كُبَّارًا

Group 3

فَإِنَّهُۥ كَانَ   لِعِبَادِهِۦ لَبَغَوْاْ

Reflect

You may have noticed that in Group 1, every example contains one of the long vowel letters (ا و ى) known as letters of *madd*. In each case they are pronounced for a duration of two counts or *harakāt*. This is the natural pronunciation for a long vowel letter.

In the chapter entitled 'Stop Sounds' (see page 30), you may recall that when you stop on a letter that carries a *fathatayn* (ً), it is pronounced as if one *fathah* has been removed and replaced with the letter *alif* (ا). In Group 2, you may have noticed all the examples follow this case, and that the last letter is pronouced with a natural *madd* duration of two counts.

Exceptions

Exceptions to the hā madd rule occur only in Surah Zumar: 7 and Surah Furqaan: 69.

In Group 3, you may have noticed that every example contains a word with the pronoun *hā* (ه) at the end of it. You may also have noticed that this *hā* (ه) is pronounced with a natural *madd* length of two counts. This only occurs when this *hā* carries a *kasrah* (ِه) or *dhummah* (ُه) and is positioned between two vowel-letters (i.e. not a *madd* letter or *sukoon*).

Rule

The *madd* letters (ا، و، ى) are pronounced with their natural length of two counts. The same rule also applies when stopping on a letter carrying *fathatayn* (ً). The pronoun letter *hā* (ه) which occurs at the end of a word is also naturally pronounced for a duration of two counts. This only occurs when this *hā* carries a *kasrah* (ه) or *dhummah* (ه) and is positioned between two vowel-letters (i.e. not a *madd* letter or *sukoon*).

Task

Search the Quran for examples of a natural *madd* of two counts. Categorise your results in the table below.

Long Vowel	Stop on Fathatayn	Pronoun Haa

Practice

Recite the verses below taking care to pronounce the natrual *madd* correctly.

﴿ ۞ وَلَوْ بَسَطَ ٱللَّهُ ٱلرِّزْقَ لِعِبَادِهِۦ لَبَغَوْاْ فِى ٱلْأَرْضِ وَلَـٰكِن يُنَزِّلُ بِقَدَرٍ مَّا يَشَآءُ إِنَّهُۥ بِعِبَادِهِۦ خَبِيرٌۢ بَصِيرٌ ﴿٢٧﴾ ﴾

Line 1

﴿ وَإِنِّى كُلَّمَا دَعَوْتُهُمْ لِتَغْفِرَ لَهُمْ جَعَلُوٓاْ أَصَـٰبِعَهُمْ فِىٓ ءَاذَانِهِمْ وَٱسْتَغْشَوْاْ ثِيَابَهُمْ وَأَصَرُّواْ وَٱسْتَكْبَرُواْ ٱسْتِكْبَارًا ﴿٧﴾ ﴾

Line 2

Study

Listen and repeat each of the following words:

Group 1

قَالُوٓاْ ءَامَنَّا	وَفِىٓ أَنفُسِكُمۡ	يَـٰٓأَيُّهَا

Group 2

يُؤَدِّهِۦٓ إِلَيۡكَ	مَالَهُۥٓ أَخۡلَدَهُۥ	وَثَاقَهُۥٓ أَحَدُ

Group 3

تُكَذِّبَانِ	مُجۡرِمُونَ	ٱلۡمُحۡسِنِينَ

Reflect

Madd Symbol

Notice that a madd symbol sometimes appears wherever a madd is optional.

Changing Lengths

Whichever madd length you choose, it should be maintained throughout a given recitation. Mixing should not occur between different optional madd lengths.

In Group 1, you may have noticed that the *madd* letter occurs at the end of a word and is followed by the letter *hamza* at the beginning of the following word. In this instance, the *madd* letter can be pronounced at its natural length of two counts or prolonged for four counts.

You may recall from the previous chapter that when the pronoun *hā* (ه) occurs at the end of a word, it is pronounced with a normal *madd* length of two counts. In Group 2, you may have noticed that the pronoun *hā* (ه) is followed by a *hamza* in the next word. In this instance, the *hā* (ه) may be pronounced for two, four or six counts. Like in the previous case, this only occurs when this *hā* carries a *kasrah* (ه) or *dhummah* (ه) and is positioned between two vowel-letters (i.e. not a *madd* letter or *sukoon*).

In Group 3, you may have noticed that the *madd* letters preceed the last letter on which the recitation stops. In this case, the *madd* letter can be pronounced at its natural length of two counts or prolonged for four or six counts. It is important to understand that this rule only applies to the word on which your recitation stops. This will most likely occur at the end of a verse, but may also occur in the middle of a verse too.

Rule

The optional *madd* of two, four or six counts occurs on three occasions:

- *Madd* letter at the end of one word followed by *hamza* at the beginning of the next word.
- The pronoun *hā* (ه) at the end of one word, followed by a *hamza* at the beginning of the next word.
- Stopping on a letter preceded by a long vowel.

Task

Search the Quran for examples of a optional *madd*. Categorise your results below.

Hamza Next Word	Ha & Hamza	Word End

Practice

Recite the verses below taking care to pronounce the optional *madd* correctly.

Line 1

﴿ وَإِلَـٰهُكُمْ إِلَـٰهٌ وَٰحِدٌ ۖ لَّآ إِلَـٰهَ إِلَّا هُوَ ٱلرَّحْمَـٰنُ ٱلرَّحِيمُ ﴿١٦٣﴾ ۞ ﴾

Line 2

﴿ وَجَعَلْنَا ٱلَّيْلَ لِبَاسًا ﴿١٠﴾ وَجَعَلْنَا ٱلنَّهَارَ مَعَاشًا ﴿١١﴾ وَبَنَيْنَا فَوْقَكُمْ سَبْعًا شِدَادًا ﴿١٢﴾ وَجَعَلْنَا سِرَاجًا وَهَّاجًا ﴿١٣﴾ ۞ ﴾

Compulsory Madd

Study

Listen and repeat each of the following words:

Group 1		
طَآئِفَةٌ	عَآئِلًا	جَآءَ

Group 2		
ٱلضَّآلِّينَ	دَآبَّةٍ	تُحَآجُّونَ

Group 3		
الٓمٓ	طسٓمٓ	كٓهيعٓصٓ

Reflect

You may have noticed that in Group 1 every word contains a *madd* letter that is followed by the letter *hamza*. The *madd* letter must be stretched for four or five counts in this instance.

Note

Notice that a madd symbol appears wherever there is a compulsory madd.

In Group 2, the *madd* letter is followed by *shaddah* (ـّ) in the same word. The *madd* letter must be stretched for six counts in this instance.

In Group 3, you may have noticed that all the examples are from the beginning of chapters from the Noble Quran that begin with seperated letters. These letters are either pronounced normally or stretched for six counts. In order to determine whether a letter is to be stretched, imagine the letter being spelt out. If its spelling contains a *madd* letter not followed by a *hamza*, it must be stretched for six counts. If this is not the case, the letter is not stretched.

Rule

Compulsory *madd* counts occur on three occasions:

- *Madd* letter followed by *hamza* (ء) in the same word (four or five counts).
- *Madd* letter followed by *shaddah* (ّ) in the same word (six counts).
- Individual letters at the beginning of a surah that contain a *madd* letter not followed by a *hamza* (six counts).

Task

Search the Quran for examples of a compulsory *madd*. Categorise your results below.

Hamza	Shaddah	Beginning Letters

Practice

Recite the verses below taking care to pronounce the compulsory *madd* correctly.

Line 1   ﴿ فَبِأَيِّ ءَالَآءِ رَبِّكُمَا تُكَذِّبَانِ ۝ ﴾

Line 2   ﴿ ٱلْحَآقَّةُ ۝ ﴾

Line 3   ﴿ حٓمٓ ۝ ﴾

Line 4   ﴿ الٓرٰ تِلْكَ ءَايَتُ ٱلْكِتَبِ ٱلْحَكِيمِ ۝ ﴾

Glossary

الضمة	Dhummah	A short vowel which generates an 'o' sound when carried by a letter.
الفتحة	Faṭḥah	A short vowel which generates an 'a' sound when carried by a letter.
غنّة	Ghunnah	A nasal sound generated when pronouncing combinations of the letters *noon*, *meem* and *tanween*.
حَرَكات	Harakāt	Plural of *harakah*.
حَرَكة	Harakah	The name given to a short vowel (*faṭḥah*, *dhummah* and *kasrah*). *Harakah* also refers to the duration of the length of time taken to pronounce a short vowel. A short vowel is counted as one *harakah*, and a long vowel is counted as two *harakāt*. For this reason, the word *harakah* is used interchangeably with the word *count* in this book.
الإدغام	Idghām	The merging of two sounds into one.
الإخفاء	Ikhfā	The concealment of one letter sound behind another during pronounciation.
الإقلاب	Iqlāb	The changing of the letter *bā* to the letter *meem* when it occurs after a *noon sākin* or *tanween*.
الاٴتعلاء	Isti'lā'	A characteristic of a letter where the tongue is raised to the roof of the mouth during pronounciation.
الاستنفال	Istinfāl	A characteristic of a letter where the tongue is kept relatively low in the mouth during pronounciation. *Istinfāl* is the opposite characteristic of *Isti'lā'*.
الاطباق	Itbāq	A characteristic of a letter where the mouth puckers during pronounciation.
إظهار	Ith-hār	The clear and normal pronounciation of a letter, free from the *ghunnah* sound.

الكسرة	*Kasrah*	A short vowel which generates an 'e' sound when carried by a letter.
المدّ	*Madd*	The elongation or stretching of a long vowel letter.
مخارج	*Makhārij*	Plural of *makhraj.*
مخرج	*Makhraj*	The location in the voice passage from where sounds originate.
المصحف	*Mus-haf*	A printed copy of the Noble Quran.
المتجانسين	*Mutajaanisayn*	Letters of the same *makhraj* but different *sifāt.*
المتماثلين	*Mutamāthilayn*	The same letter occurring twice.
المتقاربين	*Mutaqāribayn*	The merging of two letters of proximity.
الساكن	*Sākin*	The attribute given to a letter that carries a *sukoon* symbol.
الشدّة	*Shaddah*	A symbol that occurs on top of letters indicating the doubling of a letter.
الشفوي	*Shafawi*	Related to the lips.
الصفات	*Sifāt*	The characteristics of a letter.
السكون	*Sukoon*	A symbol that occurs on top of letters indicating the absence of any vowel sound on the letter.
السورة	*Sūrah*	A chapter of the Noble Quran.
التجويد	*Tajweed*	The study of the correct manner of recitation of the Noble Quran.
تَفْخِيم	*Takhfeem*	The heavy sound of a letter.
التنوين	*Tanween*	A symbol indicating the doubling of the sound of a short vowel.
تَرْقِيق	*Tarqeeq*	The light sound of a letter.

Answers

Makharij
Page 10
Task: Diagram to be completed in accordance with the table provided in the Rules section.

Throat
Page 13
Task: Diagram to be completed in accordance with the table provided in the Rules section.

Lips
Page 15
Task: Diagram to be completed in accordance with the table provided in the Rules section.

Makharij Summary
Page 21
Task: See top table on left.

Seeking Refuge
Page 23
Quick Question: Another version of the wording for seeking refuge is:

أَعُوذُ بِاللهِ السَّمِيعِ العَلِيمِ مِنَ الشَّيْطَانِ الرَّجِيمِ

Task: Any appropriate suggestion would be a valid answer for the benefits of seeking refuge.

Basmalah
Page 25
Task: It is not allowed to connect the basmalah to the last verse of a chapter and then stop before reciting the first verse of the next chapter. This is because the basmalah is associated with the beginning of a chapter and not the end of one.

Stop Symbols
Page 28
Task: Symbols and meanings will differ according to the conventions used in different *masāhif*.

Stop Sounds
Page 32
Task: Each word is rendered exactly the same as in the first column, with the only difference being a sukoon symbol that replaces the existing harakah on the last letter of the word.

Tafkheem & Tarqeeq
Page 37
Task: The letters laam and raa are not mentioned.
Page 38
Task: Table is completed in accordance with the information provided in the Rules section.

Lam Rules
Page 41
Task: Students to find their own valid examples from the Noble Quran.

Ra Rules
Page 44
Task: Students to find their own valid examples from the Noble Quran.

Qalqalah
Page 47
Task 1: The answer is to be found in the rule that follows.
Task 2: Students to find their own valid examples from the Noble Quran.

Ghunnah
Page 51
Task: Students to find their own valid examples from the Noble Quran.

Noon Saakin & Tanween
Page 52
Quick Question: Tanween is pronounced just as a noon saakin would be.
Page 55
Task: Students to find their own valid examples from the Noble Quran.

Meem Sakin
Page 57
Task: Students to find their own valid examples from the Noble Quran.

Idgham
Page 60
Task: Students to find their own valid examples from the Noble Quran.

Rules of Hamza
Page 64
Task: See bottom table on left.

Natural Madd
Page 67
Task: Students to find their own valid examples from the Noble Quran.

Optional Madd
Page 69
Task: Students to find their own valid examples from the Noble Quran.

Compulsory Madd
Page 71
Task: Students to find their own valid examples from the Noble Quran.

Makhaarij Summary Table (Page 21)

Reigon	Specific Makhraj	Letters
Chest	Chest (Long Vowels)	ا و ى
Throat	Lower throat.	ء ه
	Middle of throat.	ع ح
	Upper throat.	غ خ
Tongue	Extreme back of the tongue when touching the palate.	ق
	Back of the tongue when touching the palate.	ك
	Middle of the tongue when touching palate.	ج ش ي
	Back edge of the tongue, upturned as it touches the molar teeth.	ض
	Between the edge of the tongue when it touches the gums behind the incisors, canines and pre-molar teeth.	ل
	Between the tip of the tongue when it touches the gums behind the central incisors.	ن
	The tip of the tongue, with the top of the tip close to the gums behind the central incisors.	ر
	The tip of the tongue along with its upper surface touching the roots of the central incisors.	ط د ت
	Between the tip of the tongue and the plates near the central incisors	ص س ز
	The tip of the tongue when touching the bottom edge of the central incisors.	ث ذ ظ
Lips	Between the lips.	ب م و
	Inside-lower lip.	ف
Nasal Passage	Nasal Passage	غنّة
Total	17	

Sun and Moon Letters Table (Page 64)

Sun Letters				Moon Letters			
ض	ت	د	ط	ف	ج	ب	ق
ل	ز	س	ص	ع	ح	ء	ك
ن	ث	ذ	ظ	غ	خ	ه	
ر	م	ش	ي				
و							

Notes